# GOOGLE PIXEL 8 AND 8 PRO USER GUIDE

Detailed Manual with Comprehensive Illustration on How to Setup and Use the Google Pixel 8 & 8 Pro (Android 14 Manual) With Tips and Tricks for Beginner and Senior

D1738060

# SCOTT WHETZEL

# Table of Contents

# INTRODUCTION

The new Pixel 8 devices appear to be relatively identical to their predecessors, with a few noticeable variations. It is easier to operate the regular Pixel 8 with one hand because it is a tiny bit smaller. In contrast, the Pro model boasts a new matte appearance, sharper cameras, and an interesting temperature sensor.

Along with the upgraded Assistant and seven years of Android & security updates, the company's Tensor G3 engine is also included in the new 8 series devices. As a result, you will be able to use your gadget for longer periods compared to the previous versions

There is also an upgrade in the camera with lots of new features such as the Pro mode, video boost, enhanced color grading, night sight video and lots more

With the new generative Ai with assistant you will be able to do lots more task such as call screening, translation, transcribing etc

This book guide will walk you through the settings, setup, tips and tricks for easy understanding

# New features on Pixel 8 series

## Temperature sensor

The innovative temperature sensor on the 8 Pro device is located on the camera bar, the temperature sensor is located below the flash (the standard Pixel 8 does not have this). You must open the new Temperature app and choose the kind of object you want to measure before you can take a reading. The measurement or reading appeared on the app in a matter of seconds, and all of the outcomes appeared to be accurate.

## Utilize temperature sensor application for measurement

1. access or navigate to the temperature sensor application
2. Choose your subject
3. Place the sensor two inches or less from the object you are measuring. (The sensor is situated next to the cameras on the rear of the handset)

4. At that point, all that is needed to begin measuring is to tap the screen.

## A new generative AI with an Assistant

It should come as no surprise that Google is including such features in its phones given the popularity of generative AI this year. You'll be able to ask the Assistant to paraphrase, read aloud, and translate publications and online pages on the Pixel 8 series.

This new technology suggests activities like "Summarize," "Read aloud," "Translate," and "Search screen" once you have launched the AI Assistant.

**Note: A box with settings for playback speed, skipping forward or back 10 seconds, and a progress meter that you may move displays when you ask the Assistant to read anything out**

You may also ask the Assistant to translate articles from foreign languages into ones you understand by using the little translate icon located at the bottom right of the playback box. The Assistant can also read aloud articles in supported languages.

# Call Screening

This enables you to touch the Assistant to determine who is phoning you and why. Updates to the Pixel 8 series will make the artificial voice sound more realistic by including pauses and nonverbal cues to make it appear more genuine.

# The Recorder app

Your transcripts can soon be summarized by the Recorder app, one of my favorite Pixel-first tools. If you routinely record meetings and interviews, this can help you discover the conversation you are looking for.

# Cameras

In addition to game-changing editing features, the Pixel device 8 series includes strong, improved camera systems for exceptional photo and video quality. The 8 Pro's cameras have all been improved, starting with the primary camera, which now takes better pictures and movies in low light.

The 48-megapixel ultrawide camera in the 8 Pro is crisper, while the 48-megapixel telephoto sensor has a lens with a better f/2.8 aperture but a (slightly) broader field of vision than last year. Google claims that its f/1.68 lens has "2X optical quality" compared to last year's f/1.85 glass, but its primary camera still has the same 50MP configuration as before. The primary camera on the regular 8 is identical to that of the 8 Pro, which is marginally superior to the Pixel 8's. Its additional back sensor is essentially the same as that of the previous version

Google's camera app has undergone redesigning to make manual adjustments more accessible. There are two buttons at the bottom of the new layout that let you choose between photo and video capturing. Given that Pixels has several options, such as Action for adding motion blur to your images

Google has also included a Pro mode that allows you to manually adjust the brightness, shadow, and white balance settings as well as take still photos with a 50-megapixel resolution.

**Note: To activate Manual mode, navigate to the settings menu. Doing so will disable the automatic lens change option.**

The basic Pixel 8 now supports macro photography for the first time, and it has the same capabilities as the Pixel 8 Pro. The Pro model from this year can operate up to two cm away.

The Pixel 8's cameras include some of the most significant upgrades in video recording and processing. The biggest new function is Video Boost, which will upload your videos to the cloud so that Google's more potent processing units can improve them. These include the use of HDR+, improved color grading, and Night Sight Video for the first time.

However, I'm more interested in what Google refers to as "Audio Magic Eraser." This new tool can decrease background noise in your movies, much as the Magic Eraser for pictures can get rid of background photobombers. Magic Editor, will also be accessible. The 10.5MP selfie camera in the Pixel 8 Pro finally has autofocus, while the 10.5MP selfie sensor on the Pixel 8 has fixed focus.

# Displays, face unlock, & other upgrades

Face Unlock, for instance, may now be used in additional contexts, such as verifying mobile payments or logging into applications, since it has been determined to match the company's internal security criteria. The Tensor G3 chip in both phones, which also powers applications like Audio Magic Eraser, which filters out more spam calls and other things, contributes to this in part.

Google's new designation for the displays it uses on the Pixels is Actua for the standard pixel 8 device and Super Actua for the Pro.

# Battery

There is an upgrade in the battery life and performance on the 8 series (4,585 mAh) and 8 pros (5,050 mAh) compared to the 8 series

# New pixel series Specifications

| S/N | NEW FEATURES | PIXEL 8 | PIXEL 8 PRO |
|---|---|---|---|
| 1 | Processor | Google Tensor G3 | Google Tensor G3 |
| 2 | Software | Android 14 | Android 14 |
| 3 | Display size, tech, resolution, refresh rate, brightness | 6.2-inch OLED; 2,400x1,080 pixels; 60 120Hz adaptive refresh rate | 6.8-inch OLED; 3,120x1,440 pixels; 1-120Hz adaptive refresh rate |
| 4 | Front-facing camera | 10.5-megapixel | 10.5-megapixel |
| 5 | Camera | 50-megapixel (wide), 12-megapixel (ultrawide) | 50-megapixel (wide), 48-megapixel (ultrawide), 48-megapixel (telephoto) |
| 6 | Video capture | 4K | 4K |
| 8 | Storage and | 8GB + 128GB, | 12GB RAM + |

|    |                            |                  |                              |
| -- | -------------------------- | ---------------- | ---------------------------- |
|    | RAM                        | 256GB            | 128GB, 256GB, 512GB, 1TB     |
| 8  | Fingerprint sensor         | Under display    | Under display                |
| 9  | Connector                  | USB-C            | USB-C                        |
| 10 | Battery                    | 4,585 mAh        | 5,050 mAh                    |
| 11 | Pixel density              | 428 ppi          | 489 ppi                      |
| 12 | Weight (grams, ounces)     | 188 g (6.6 oz)   | 213 g (8.5 oz)               |
| 13 | Price                      | $699 (128GB) £585 (128GB) | FOR US: $999 (128GB) FOR UK: £825 (128GB) |

# CHAPTER 1

# Toggle off/on your gadget

Now that you have gotten a new pixel gadget, check out the basic toggling on-and-off setup for your gadget

## Turn on your gadget

When your phone is off,

1. Touch & hold the Power knob (button) for a sec to switch on your gadget

2. Input a passphrase to access your gadget

# Toggle off your gadget

If you must shut down your Gadget, do so via

1. hold down and hit on the power or unlock knob on your gadget when it is locked or unlocked pending when a display with numerous options shows

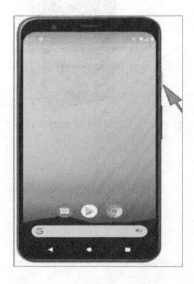

2. We choose "Power off" from the list of options on the gadget's screen. Accept any confirmation messages that may occur

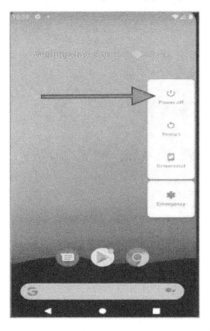

3. Wait a few seconds or minutes for the gadget to completely shut down once the screen goes black. Once it is toggled back on, it requests for the passphrase used such as pattern, thumbprint, or code in addition to the SIM card's PIN code.

## When the assistant is not activated or the power button on the Pixel 8 Pro is not functional.

1. We start by displaying your Google Pixel 8 Pro's quick access or settings bar. The shortcuts to the device settings will be visible if you swipe your finger from the top of the screen downward when the Google Pixel 8 Pro is unlocked.

2. Swipe again to completely open the shortcuts panel in the second step. The button with the on/off icon will be in the lower right corner; click on it to proceed.

3. Activating emergency mode, rebooting, and the choice we're searching for: "Turn off" will all be available on the Pixel 8 Pro screen in the third step. To carry on, hit on the **Turn Off** knob

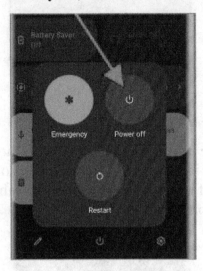

# CHAPTER 2

# Sim-card settings

Before setting your gadget up, it is advisable to insert your sim before toggling your device on or set esim up while turning it on. In this chapter, we will explain setting up all about sim card

# Insert (Add) or Remove a SIM Card

A No SIM message will appear on the lock screen and in expanded quick settings when there is no SIM card inserted in the smartphone.

# Find the SIM tray

1. On the left side of the smartphone is where you'll find the SIM tray.
2. A SIM tool must be inserted into the tiny hole to expel the SIM tray to insert a SIM.

# Adding or taking out the SIM

- Push the tool tightly but softly pending when the tray comes out
- Take out the tray.
- Insert the nano SIM with the SIM connection module facing up in the slot.
- Input the tray again into its opening tenderly. The SIM card will then be immediately read by your phone.

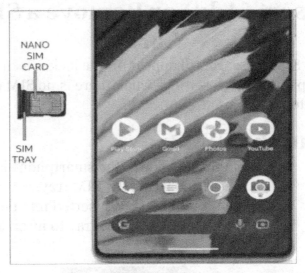

NANO
SIM
CARD

SIM
TRAY

# Use two eSim profiles

To make two eSim profiles available on your qualified device:

1. Navigate to and hit on your setup (Settings) application via your gadget
2. Then choose SIMs under Network & Internet
3. Instead, click Download a SIM
4. Trail the directions.

## Setting the standard (default) Simcard for calling, texting, & data

1. Launch the Settings app.
2. finally, choose SIMs, followed by your network, and finally Network & internet
3. Set your choices for each network:
   - Information: Enable mobile data.
   - Important: The standard SIM for data may only be one SIM. You will receive a notice if you already have one configured.
   - Call Preference can be tapped. Choose your default carriers after that, or select Ask over every period (time)
   - Messages: Select SMS Preference. Choose your default carriers after that, or select Ask me every time.

# Remove an eSIM

1. Navigate to and hit on your setup (Settings) application via your gadget
2. Select a Mobile network from the Network & Internet menu
3. Choose the eSIM that you wish to remove
4. Select Delete SIM
5. A Passphrase will be required to erase an eSIM
6. Navigate to and hit on your setup (Settings) application via your gadget
7. Confirm SIM deletion after selecting Security, Advanced, and then Security.

# CHAPTER 3

# Setup Device

Setting up your gadget is one of the most salient things to do for you to be able to adequately utilize your gadget, this is always the first setup for your new phone, check this chapter out as we walk you through setting up your gadget

After doing a factory reset or as a first-timer, set up your device

1. You will be guided through a series of prompts to set your gadget up upon turning the device on for the first time or after a factory reset. Select Get Started to proceed after selecting the preferred language

2. To pair or link up to a Wi-Fi service (network), choose the desired network name and adhere to the on-screen instructions. Select Setup on your mobile network using the mobile network

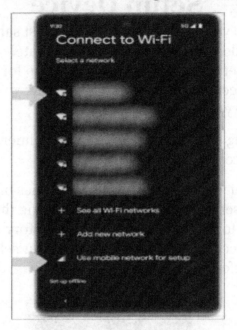

3. Select Next and follow the instructions if you want to restore data from your old handset to your new smartphone. To configure the device without restoring, choose Don't copy

4. If you want to utilize Google Services like the
   Play Store, Gmail, Google Maps, and more, you
   must log into a Google account. To add your
   Google account, enter your email address or
   phone number, then follow the on-screen
   instructions. Choose Create account if you
   don't already have one but would want to.
   Select Skip if you want to keep on without
   creating an account. Click Next to proceed

5. Examine the prompt from Google Services. Select I accept to finish configuring the device.

    3. **Only if your Google account was added will you see this screen, please note.**

6. Look over the Google services prompt before choosing the appropriate changes. After you're done, click Accept. Evaluate the Google One prompt before turning it on or off. Select I accept after carefully reading the prompt for further legal terms

7. Type the preferred PIN and choose Next if you intend to set or configure a screen display lock for security. Select Screen lock choices, then select the preferred preference & trail the televised instructions to finish the setup to secure your gadget utilizing an alternative screen lock. Hit on Skip to continue without configuring a screen lock.

4. **Note: If you choose Skip, carefully read the prompt before choosing Skip once more to proceed without configuring a screen lock. To finish configuring the device, choose Continue.**

8. Examine the prompt for fingerprint unlocking. Choose No Thanks to go without setting up Fingerprint Lock or choose I agree to set up Fingerprint Lock.

9. Examine the prompt for face unlocking. Choose No Thanks to go without setting up Fingerprint Lock or choose I agree to set up Fingerprint Lock

10. Examine the prompt to continue setup. To continue configuring your device, select Continue. Choose Leave & Get reminder if you want to go forward without setting up your gadget

11. Go through the "Hey Google" prompt to talk to Google hands-free. Choose I agree to install Google Assistant, or choose Skip to proceed without installing it
12. Go through the screen that says "Access your Assistant without unlocking your device." Choose I accept to give Google Assistant permission to utilize the lock screen or choose Skip to go without it.
13. Read the instructions to Check out quickly using your phone. Choose Next to activate Google Pay, or choose Skip to proceed without it
14. Choose the desired choice and follow the on-screen instructions if you want to add a new email account, listen to music nearby, alter the background or text size, explore more programs, or manage the information displayed on the lock screen. Select No Thanks to proceed without configuring any other things
15. Look over the offer to "Get more tips & tricks in your inbox" and click "No thanks" or "Yes, I'm in."
16. After carefully reading the gesture prompt, choose Try it and follow the instructions. When done, choose Done
17. To complete setting up, slide upward via the lower section of the display screen.

# CHAPTER 4

# Charging your gadget

Once you have been able to successfully set up your sim card and gadget, the next important thing to take note of is the battery level or percentage

Right in this chapter you will learn how to charge your gadget the standard way or wirelessly

## Charging your gadget

- The power adapter and USB cord that comes with your phone should be plugged into the opposite end of the cord.

- Plug or connect your adapter to an electric outlet
- At the top of your smartphone, next to the battery symbol, there will be a charging indicator.

# Charging wirelessly

Using a Pixel Stand, you may wirelessly charge your phone.

You may use your Pixel Stand to charge Qi-certified mobile devices.

1. Make sure your Pixel phone stand is hooked to a power source and connected to the included power adapter before you start.

   - Place your phone on the Pixel Stand's center shelf with the screen facing outward.

- **Note: Pixel Stand is an optional purchase.**

2. Tap Next to connect your Pixel phone to your Pixel Stand.

- **Note: Tap No thanks to forego configuring your Pixel Stand**

3. Tap Turn on if you want to be able to operate connected devices, such as smart lighting or your thermostat, while your phone is being

charged on your Pixel Stand. You may also press No thanks to set up later.

4. Your experience can be tailored by Google Assistant. Tap Next to start using Google Assistant when your device is in the Pixel Stand.

- **Note: Tap No thanks if you don't want to link your Google Assistant.**

5. Tap I agree to access your private information, such as images, calendar events, or emails, even if your phone's screen is locked.

- **Note: Tap No Thanks to disable personal results from your Google Assistant.**

6. Click Continue to view a slideshow of Google Photos albums while your smartphone is secured to your Pixel Stand.

- **Note: Tap No thanks if you don't wish to utilize this function.**

7. Turn on Do Not Disturb to hide all alerts when using your Pixel Stand with your phone. Next, choose Turn on.

- **Note: Tap No thanks to stop Do Not Disturb from activating while your phone is charging.**

8. Just before your morning alarm goes off, press Turn on to gradually brighten your screen.

- **Note: Tap No thanks to forego setting up Sunrise Alarm.**

9. The default charging setting on your Pixel Stand is "Optimized," which modifies both the fan noise and the pace at which your phone charges. Click Next.

- **Note: After setup, this value can be modified.**

10. Click Done.

11. After setup, go to Settings to modify your Pixel Stand's settings. Tap connected devices after that. After that, tap the Pixel Stand gadget.

12. Activate or deactivate any setting.

# CHAPTER 5

# Transfer your data

To other Android and iPhone device users who wish to switch to the new Pixel 8 series and are worried about their data, files, or documents on their gadget, here is an easy technique to move them to the new Pixel 8 gadget

## Switch to a Pixel phone from an Android one

Whatever phone you're switching from, there are a few easy steps you can take to move your data, such as images or texts, via your older handset to the new Pixel.

1. Prepare to install your new Pixel.
   Check to see whether you have the following things:
   - Your most recent version of Android OS on a fully charged phone with a charging cord
   - Your brand-new Pixel is charged.
   - The Pixel's included Quick Switch Adapter
   - an effective WiFi connection
   - The SIM Card Inserter that was included with your Pixel
2. Connect to Wi-Fi after inserting your SIM card.

3. Incorporate the phones
   - Hit on the subsequent icon (Next) once a **Copy Apps and Data** pops up

4. Copy your data

- Unmark the box after the specific data you don't wish to send. Tap Copy when you're prepared.

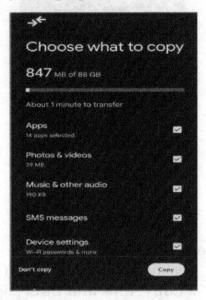

# Switch to a Pixel phone from an iPhone

1. Prepare to install your new Pixel.
   Check to see whether you have the following things:
   - Using the most recent software, a fully charged iPhone, and a charging cord
   - Your brand-new Pixel is charged.
   - The Pixel's included Quick Switch Adapter
   - an effective WiFi connection
   - The SIM Card Inserter that was included with your Pixel
2. Get your iPhone ready.

- Toggle Facetime & iMessage off via your iPhone gadget.
- Go to Settings > Messages > Turn off iMessage on your iPhone while the SIM card is still in the device.
- Follow suit with FaceTime next. Toggle FaceTime off via navigating to Settings (setups) > FaceTime.

3. Connect to Wi-Fi after inserting your SIM card.
   - You may now begin configuring your new Pixel. Tap Get Started after turning on your Pixel smartphone. The language and vision settings on your phone are editable.

4. Join the phones.
   - Hit on the subsequent icon (**Next**) once a **Copy Apps & Data** pops up

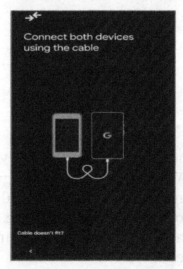

5. Copy the data
   • Uncheck the box next to the data you
     don't want to transfer if you wish to. Tap
     Copy when you're prepared.

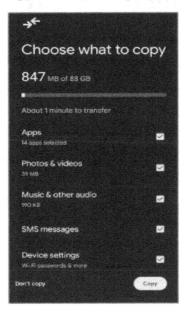

# CHAPTER 6

# Resetting or restoring your gadget

Restore from the Pixel 8 Pro's menu choices

You should adhere to these easy procedures if you wish to do a reset using the device options to restore your new gadget to its factory settings:

1. On your Google gadget, search for a cogwheel look alike to reach the settings menu. The settings menu will open when you click or hit on it.

2. The next step is to go down to the "System" section of your new Pixel 8 settings and click or press to proceed.

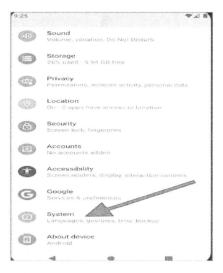

3. Select "Reset options" from this section to restore network settings, and program, or to fully reset your gadget

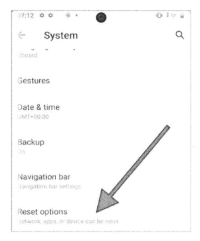

4. Hit on **wipe all data** or **data reset**" as your final preference

5. The data you have sent to Google, Twitter, Instagram, and Facebook, or copies of backups that you left in the cloud, for instance, Google Drive, Dropbox, or One Drive, won't be erased, based on the initial affirmation alerts

- The accounts connected to this Pixel 8 Pro will also be shown. IMPORTANT: before trying out a factory reset, you

must be aware of the password for the primary Google account because once you are done formatting & rebooting, the gadget will prompt you for it

- Hit on **wipe all data** via the list of preferences.

6. A second confirmation notice will show up informing you that all data on your Google Pixel 8 Pro and any program you've downloaded will be deleted and warning you that this decision cannot be reversed.

Hit on **wipe all data** if you consent to it.

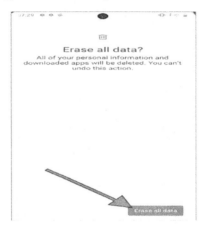

7. If required, draw the screen unlock pattern or type the PIN or password for the screen unlock to proceed.

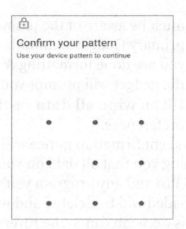

Confirm your pattern
Use your device pattern to continue

8. Your Google Pixel 8 Pro will restart and take a few minutes to start while optimizing the pre-installed Android 13 operating system program and returning the device to its factory condition.

Android is starting...

Optimizing app 1 of 1

# CHAPTER 8

# Place and Answer Calls

## Utilize in-call options

The following choices will be accessible when on an active call:

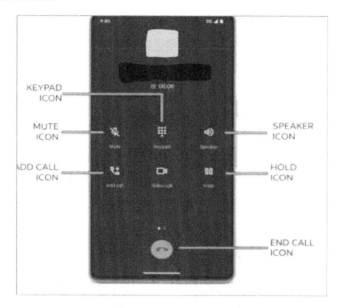

## Calling a phone number

1. Navigate to the phone application
2. Hit the phone symbol on the home screen
   - To call someone, dial their number and the area code by tapping the number pad.

# Make a phone call

1. Tap the call icon (often represented by a phone receiver) after entering the phone number to start the call.

    - You may also retrieve the number through the Contacts app or the Phone app's contact list if you have stored it in your contacts.

# Accept an incoming call

The caller's details will be shown on the screen when an incoming call is made,

- Swipe the green phone symbol to the right to answer the call.

# Reject an incoming call.

- Swipe the red phone symbol to the left to reject the incoming call.

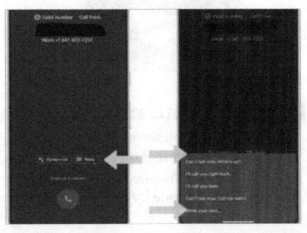

# Ending or Hanging up a call

- Tap the red phone symbol with the call active to stop the call.

## Using the Call Screen feature on a Pixel phone

You will be able to physically screen calls & read the transcription of a discussion to find out who is calling and why, saving you from missing the call.

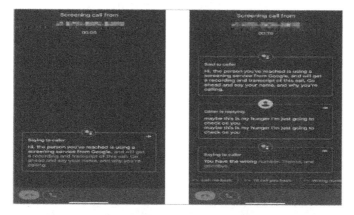

## Open or Access screen calling setup

There are a some alternative   for screen calling that allows you some control over how the AI Assistant responds to incoming unknown calls. The following is how you can get to them:

1. Navigate to and launch your Phone application
2. Press the upper-right corner's three dots
3. Select Setting
4. Select the option for the Spam & screen display Calling

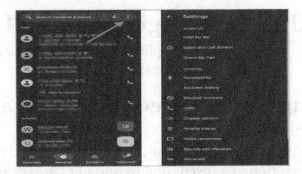

5. Allow View the spam and caller ID
6. Access the settings by opening Call Screen.

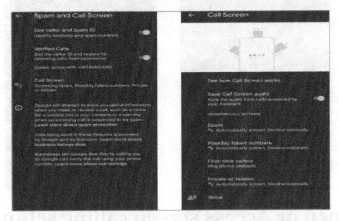

You may adjust a number of settings in this area to suit your preferences and make sure you don't miss any crucial calls.

# Utilize speakerphone

- By pressing the speaker icon on the call screen during a call, you may turn on the loudspeaker.
- Through the device's speakers, you may hear the call without holding it up to your ear.

# Mute or un-mute a call

- By pressing the mic logo on the call screen, you may silence or unmute your microphone while on a call.

# Setting call hold

- Tap the hold symbol on the call screen to place a call on hold if necessary.

By doing so, the call will be on hold and you are free to place or take another call.

# Switch between calls

When you tap the call you wish to concentrate on on the call screen, you may flip between any ongoing calls.

# Add preferred contacts

1. Choose the Contacts tab via the Phone application on your phone,

2. Then choose the appropriate contact. To add the contact to your favorites list, use the Favourite symbol.

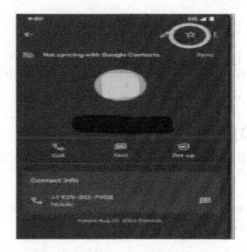

3. To view your favorite contacts, go to the
   Favorites tab in the Phone app. Pick and hit on
   the individual you intend to call and want

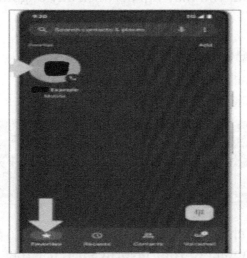

# Utilize your phone when on call

1. Swipe up from the bottom of the screen during
   on a call to get to the home display screen.

2. Swipe down from the Notifications bar and tap the active call notice to return to an active call.

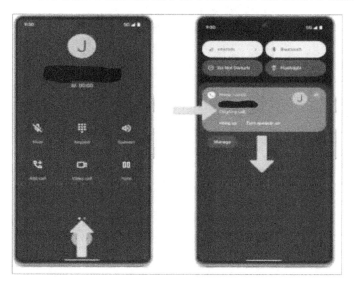

# Start or Set a conference call

1. Pick the Add call icon from an active call, then
2. Follow the on-screen instructions.
3. Select the End Call icon to end a call.

# Reject a call via text message

To decline a call and reply with a text message,

- Choose Reply when you get one.
- Choose the text message you want to send, or choose Write your own... to create your own.

# How to activate the Clear Calling feature on your Pixel

Clear Calling may be activated easily. You may go forward after turning it on.

1. launch the Settings app
2. Select Vibration & Sound

3. Slide downward
4. Hit on Clear calling
5. To turn on Clear Calling, twist the toggle.

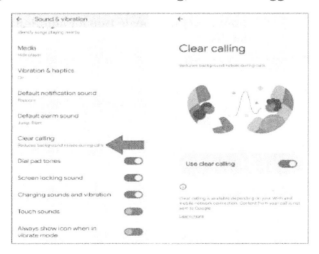

You may now clearly hear your calls because it is that easy.

# CHAPTER 8

# Making video Calls

Utilize Google (Duo) to create or generate & accept video calls.

## Install Google Duo

1. Slide upward via the middle of the display screen to reach the Apps tray via the home screen
2. Choose the Duo application.

   - **Note: You will be requested to check the Terms of Service and the Privacy Policy upon initial entry. Select I accept to proceed after selecting the preferred policy to examine. You will also be asked to provide access to your camera and mobile. Hit on Allow or consent to it to continue while utilizing the application > While utilizing the application. Navigate or move to Set up Google Duo for additional details.**

# Video call someone

1. Choose New to see the list of contacts, then hit on the preferred contact.

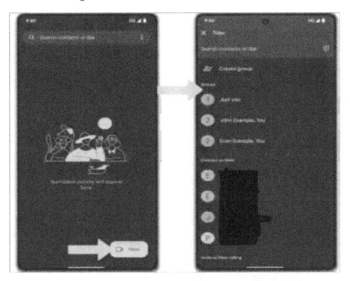

- Note. Both owners have to be logged into Google Duo in other to call. To invite a friend via Google Duo, hit on the Invite logo.

2. To begin video calling, click the Video Call button.

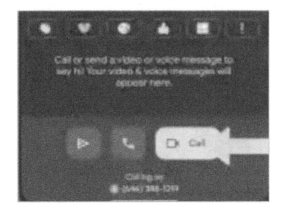

# Creating group video calling

1. Choose Create group from the contacts list. Then click Done after selecting the required contacts.

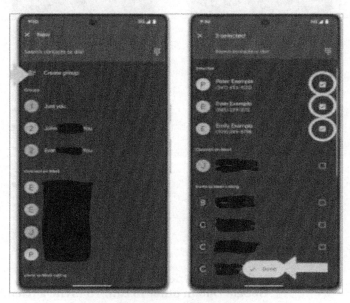

2. To create a video call, hit Start.

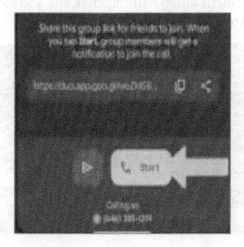

# Reject or Answer an incoming call

To attend or pick up a call,

- Hit on & slide the call icon upward or downward.

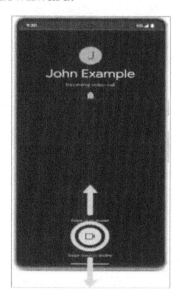

## Options for video calls

Choose the preferred choice:

- SWITCH CAMERAS: Click the symbol for switching cameras
- Click or hit on the Filters logo to use the filters.
- Slide upward via the lower section of the screen to get back to the home screen if you need to use your phone while on a video conversation. A picture-in-picture

window in the corner of your screen will
show the video call.

- Swipe down from the Notifications bar,
  then click the active call notice to return
  to a call.

# CHAPTER 9

# Internet and connectivity

One salient feature on your new pixel gadget is the internet service and connectivity, follow through as we walk you through all the necessary setups

## Setting up or Configuring your Gadgets Internet

1. This handbook will teach you how to manually configure the network or return your phone to its factory default Internet settings to set up Internet on it.
2. Slide upward via your gadget display

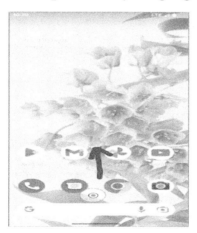

3. Navigate to and choose Settings

## 4. Pick Internet and Network

## 5. Hit on SIMs

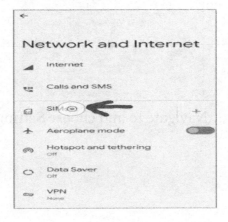

6. Scroll down to, then choose Access point names

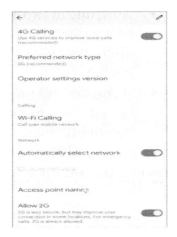

7. Choose the Menu button.

8. Choose "Reset to default"

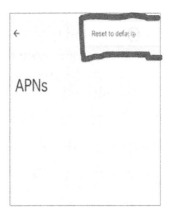

- You may restore the Internet and MMS settings on your phone.
- Now, any network issues should be resolved. Don't forget to disconnect your Wi-Fi before testing.
- If you are still unable to access the internet, please continue with the instructions.

9. Choose a new APN, and
10. provide your Internet details

11. Scroll down and type your online details
- Please take note that only the yellow-highlighted values should be altered.

12. Click on the Menu button
13. Click Save

14. Pick the Internet access point.

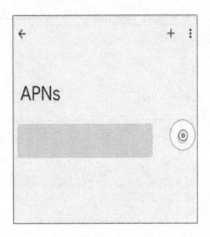

- The Internet has now been configured on your phone.

# Sharing your internet

1. First, make sure your gadget has 3G, 4G, or 5G mobile connectivity turned on. The shortcuts to the gadget setup will be visible if you swipe your finger via the upper section of the display screen downward when the gadget is unlocked

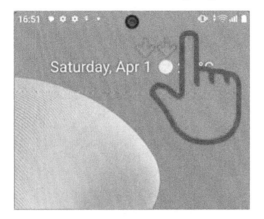

2. If the symbol for the 3G/4G/5G data connection to the internet does not already show in color, click it to toggle it on

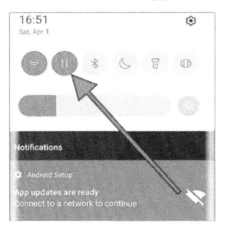

   - **If you are unable to locate the symbol in the picture, slide downward one**

65

3. Go to the device settings on your Google Pixel 8 Pro, which is the gear wheel symbol on the home display screen or in the phone menu; you may enter the main menu by dragging your finger from the bottom to the upper section of the display screen.

4. Click "Networks & internet" or "Connections" and then select "More" as the next step.

5. Click "Hotspot & tethering" in the fifth step

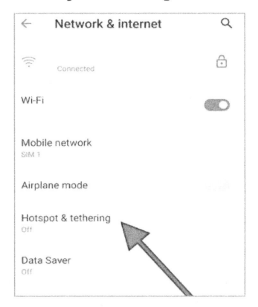

6. Set up the shared connection by setting up a Wi-Fi network that other devices may join on your pixel gadget by clicking the "Wi-Fi hotspot" section once within the "Hotspot & tethering" section.

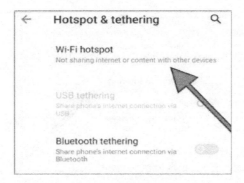

7. If the Wi-Fi access point on your Google already looks to be enabled, skip to the next step. If not, press the button in the accompanying image to activate it.

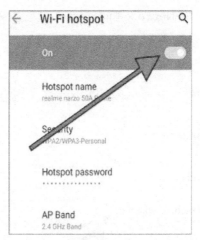

8. In the "Hotspot name" area, the designation of the Wi-Fi service or network that the Pixel 8 Pro generated using its data connection will be shown. This is the Wi-Fi network that has to be searched for and used on the other device from which you wish to connect. By clicking and modifying the name, you may alter the network's name if you wish to.

9. In the "Hotspot password" area, you will be able to find the passphrase for the Wi-Fi service or access point that the Pixel 8 Pro set.

- **To check the password and change it to a simpler or more difficult one, click on the dots or asterisks.**

10. Click "OK" to proceed after checking or updating the password.

11. Click on the "Security" area if you wish to modify the Wi-Fi access point's security settings.

12. The most recent security protocol is "WPA3-Personal"; nevertheless, you must alter it based

on whether the device you wish to connect through Wi-Fi allows such a recent protocol or an older one

13. Click "AP Band" to adjust the access point band of the access point you created with Google

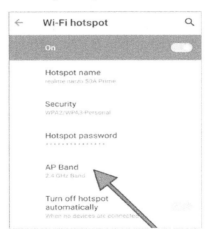

14. Depending on the software version or the location of your Pixel 8 Pro, your smartphone

may display other options in addition to the 2.4 GHz or 5 Ghz bands.

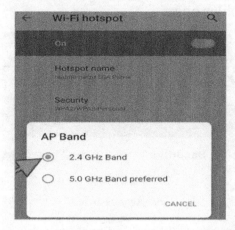

- **While the lower band (2.4 GHz) is more saturated than the higher band (5 GHz) on average, it provides a stronger connection across longer distances because other Wi-Fi networks are typically set up at this frequency.**

You may search for and set up this portable Wi-Fi network after clicking "Save" to share the internet connection from your Pixel 8 Pro with another device.

# Share the WiFi password with your gadget

On your Pixel 8 Pro, here's how to generate a QR code which includes the Wi-Fi password.

Even though Google may have gotten fresh upgrades over time, the Android operating system version it ships with is 14.

When the QR code is created on your Pixel 8 Pro, you can read it using the camera on the other device and save it as an image to use it as many times as you like without having to repeat these procedures.

1. To share or distribute a Wi-Fi service from our Google device, we must first confirm that we are connected to it. If we are, we may open the settings on the Pixel 8 Pro by tapping the icon of a gear wheel. Slide upward via the lower section of the Pixel 8 Pro home screen to see it if it is not visible there

2. The next step is to select "Networks and Internet" or "Connections" from the settings menu on the Pixel 8 Pro. To go to the Wi-Fi network settings, press it

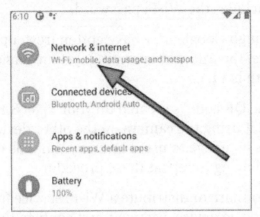

3. The Wi-Fi connection will be the first component to show up in your Google Pixel 8 Pro's network and internet settings.

- Now, try to confirm that it is paired or linked; if not, click on the symbol on the right with a single touch to activate it and make it visible in blue. After

74

4. The accessible Wi-Fi networks, both those we have set up and those we have not, will show up in a list after we enter the Wi-Fi network settings, which is the fourth step. Your Google Pixel 8 Pro is connected to the first Wi-Fi network that shows; to view more information, click the gear icon that appears to the right of the network's name.

5. You will notice a QR emblem after the designation of the wireless network on the right, along with the words "QR Code," when you view the information of the Wi-Fi network saved in your Pixel 8 Pro and whose access code you wish to share to log in from another device. To view the QR code, click it

6. The Google Pixel 8 Pro screen will display the QR code. Use the other device you wish to use to access the Wi-Fi web to scan the QR code.

- **If you don't know the methods to snap a screenshot on your Pixel 8 Pro and want to print or save the QR code for later, you may do so by snapping a photograph of the page instead.**

# Connect to Wi-Fi networks

## Toggle on & pair to the internet

1. Navigate or slide to the setup (Settings) application on your gadget
2. Select Internet, then select Network & Internet
3. Activate Wi-Fi
4. Hit a network (service) via the menu. If a password is required, the Lock symbol will appear. Once you've connected:
   - Below the network designation, "Connected" is shown.
   - The network service will be "Stored." Your gadget automatically pairs when it is in range and Wi-Fi is turned on.

## Adding a saved (service) network

**Option 1;** is to await a reload of the network list.

Pause for some seconds so the menu will be able to refresh if the network you seek is closed but not listed.

**Option 2:** Include network

1. Navigate or slide to the setup (Settings) application on your gadget
2. Select Internet, then select Network & Internet
3. Be certain to toggle the Wi-Fi on
4. Tap Add Network via the lower section of the menu

5. Input the network designation (SSID) and security information as necessary
6. Click Save.

## Remove a saved network

1. Navigate or slide to the setup (Settings) application on your gadget
2. Select Internet, then select Network & Internet
3. Be certain to toggle the Wi-Fi on
4. Touch and hold a network you've saved
5. Click Forget.

## Setting up OpenRoaming

It's important to note that you can only configure OpenRoaming when within range of an OpenRoaming network. Your phone will automatically connect to any nearby OpenRoaming networks after setup.

For your Pixel phone's OpenRoaming configuration:

You will have to Launch Set-up apps as explained below

## Launch Set-up apps on your Pixel 8

1. Select Internet, then select Network & Internet
2. Tap an OpenRoaming network in the Wi-Fi list if you are within range of it
3. Evaluate the rules & conditions displayed on the screen. Select Continue
4. To authenticate, hit on the Google account you want to use.

# Disable or alter OpenRoaming's settings

The account you utilize for OpenRoaming might be disconnected, forgotten, or changed.

1. Navigate or slide to the setup (Settings) application on your gadget when linked to an OpenRoaming hotspot.
2. Select Internet, then hit on Network service & Internet.
3. Tap Settings next to "OpenRoaming."
4. Tap Disconnect to leave the particular hotspot
5. Tap Forget to prevent connecting to OpenRoaming once again
6. Tap Advanced and then Subscription to alter the OpenRoaming account you use.

# Joining wireless networks

1. Turn On and connect
2. Navigate or slide to the setup (Settings) application on your gadget
3. Select Internet, then select Network & Internet
4. Activate Wi-Fi
5. Hit a network (service) via the menu. If a password is required, the Lock symbol will appear. Once you've connected:
   - Under the network name, "Connected" is shown
   - The network service will be "Stored." Your device automatically connects when it is in range and Wi-Fi is turned on.

# Switch on nearby saved networks automatically

1. Navigate or slide to the setup (Settings) application on your gadget
2. Select Internet, then Network Preferences, then Network & Internet
3. Wi-Fi will immediately turn on. Activate Location services first, then Location if necessary
4. Activate Bluetooth and Wi-Fi scanning.

# Modify, add, distribute, or delete stored networks

Modify a network you've stored

1. Navigate or slide to the setup (Settings) application on your gadget
2. Toggle Internet & Network. Then came Wi-Fi
3. Tap a network name to switch between the listed networks
4. Tap the network to modify its settings.

# Adding a saved network

**Option 1;** is to await a reload of the network list.

Wait for the list to refresh if the network service you seek is close but not listed.

**Option** 2: adding network

1. Navigate or slide to the setup (Settings) application on your gadget
2. Select Internet, then hit on Network service & Internet

3. Be certain to toggle the Wi-Fi on
4. Tap Add Network via the lower section of the menu
5. Input the network or service designation (name (SSID) & security information as necessary
6. Click Save.

# Control sophisticated network configurations

1. To connect devices, configure a proxy
2. Navigate or slide to the setup (Settings) application on your gadget
3. Toggle Internet & Network. Internet comes next
4. Use a network tap
5. Hit on Advanced setups via the Editing option
6. Select "Proxy," then click the Down arrow. Select a configuration type
7. Enter the proxy settings if necessary
8. Click Save.

# Utilize metered Wi-Fi to regulate data use

Wi-Fi-connect your smartphone or tablet

1. Navigate or Slide to the Settings application on your gadget
2. Select Internet from the Network & Internet menu.
3. You will be able to pair to a Wi-Fi service by tapping it.
4. Then choose Network utilization. Consider as metered.

# CHAPTER 10

# Bluetooth

Find out how to unpair a paired device, and toggle Bluetooth on/off.

## Turning Bluetooth on/off shortcut

To toggle Bluetooth on or off,

1. Swipe down from the notification bar and click the Bluetooth icon.

## Activate or deactivate Bluetooth

1. Use two fingers to swipe down from the Notification bar, then click the Settings button.
2. Choose Bluetooth under Connected devices > Connection preferences. To toggle Bluetooth on/ off, use the Bluetooth switch.

# Pairing your gadget with a device

1. Choose Pair new device from the Bluetooth screen in step one.

2. A device search is initiated by your device. Choose the required gadget. When prompted to initiate a pairing, choose Pair.

# Unpair your gadget

1. Click the Settings icon next to the appropriate device on the Connected devices screen
2. To disconnect the gadget, choose Forget. To confirm, choose Forget device.

# CHAPTER 11

# Using a hotspot or tethering to share a mobile connection

## Add extra Wi-Fi setup changes

1. Navigate or slide to the setup (Settings) application on your gadget
2. Toggle Internet & Network. Internet comes next
3. Then choose Network Preferences
4. Tap a choice. These depend on the kind of Android and the device

## Using Bluetooth to tether

1. Pair your handset to the other device.
2. Configure the other device so that it may connect to the network through Bluetooth. Check out the roadmap offered with the equipment
3. Slide to the setup (Settings) app on your handset
4. Toggle Internet & Network. Then comes tethering and hotspot
5. Select Bluetooth tethering.

# USB cable tethering

Pair your handset to a new device via a USB cord. At the upper section of the display screen, a notice titled **Connected** appears.

1. Navigate or slide to the setup (Settings) application on your gadget
2. Select Hotspot & tethering after selecting Network & internet
3. Activate USB tethering.

# Auto-shutdown your hotspot

Your hotspot will switch off whenever you do not have any devices connected to conserve battery life.

1. Navigate or slide to the setup (Settings) application on your gadget
2. Select Wi-Fi hotspot by tapping Network & internet, Hotspot & tethering, and finally
3. Tap switch off hotspot automatically to switch this option on or off.

# Chapter 12

# Lock the screen

Your new gadget is designed to be able to lock your gadget via facial recognition, fingerprint, and the use of a passphrase

To further safeguard your Android smartphone or tablet, you may configure a screen lock if you want to.

Check how the how-to below

# Activate or modify a screen lock

1. Launch the Settings app.
2. Then select Security & settings
3. Tap Screen lock to select a certain type of screen lock.
4. Before you can select a different lock if you've previously established one, you'll need to enter your PIN, pattern, or password
5. Select the screen lock option by tapping it. Follow or trail the directives displayed on the screen
6. Next to "Screen lock," tap Settings to modify your screen lock's settings. Lock screen test, Power button (knob) locking, & automatic lock time is among the settings.

# Set up fingerprint authentication

1.  Open the Settings app and select Security & privacy to configure a fingerprint for your Pixel

2.  Device lock, tap. Tap Facial & Fingerprint Unlock after that

3. You will be prompted to enter a backup Pincode, pattern, or passphrase if you don't already have a screen lock configured.

4. Click Fingerprint Unlock under "Ways to unlock."

5. Review the operation of Fingerprint Unlock for a minute. When done, scroll down and choose I agree

6. You'll be asked to configure your fingerprint on the next screen. Press Start.

7. Touch the sensor with your finger and hold it pending when the sensor lights up and your device vibrates

8. Each time the fingerprint symbol changes, lift your finger, then press and hold it on the sensor. Each time, adjust your finger's location

a little bit, being sure to press the sides of your finger against the sensor when instructed

9. Tap Done when your fingerprint has been uploaded.

You may also add more fingerprints if you want to unlock your device with your other hands or fingers.

# Managing fingerprint settings

## Delete or rename the prints you made

1. Navigate or slide to the setup (Settings) application on your gadget
2. Then select Device Lock, followed by Facial & Fingerprint Unlock, Device Lock, and finally Fingerprint Unlock
3. Utilize your backup display screen lock technique or scan your existing fingerprint.
4. Make the desired changes
5. Now, select Delete fingerprint to remove it.
6. By tapping a fingerprint, entering a new name, and then tapping OK, you may rename it.

# Disable the use and remove fingerprints

**Option 1: Only use a password, pattern, or PIN to unlock**

Remove your fingerprint to utilise your backup display screen lock Pincode or pattern:

1. Navigate or slide to the setup (Settings) application on your gadget
2. Select Security.
3. Then select Device Lock, followed by Facial & Fingerprint Unlock, Device Lock, and finally Fingerprint Unlock
4. Utilize your Pincode, pattern, or passphrase, or scan your fingerprint

5. Tap Delete after a fingerprint. Do this for each fingerprint.

**Option 2: Disable the phone's screen lock security**

For security reasons, we firmly advise keeping your screen locked. However, if you'd prefer not to use your fingerprint, a PIN, a pattern, a password, or a Smart Lock:

1. Navigate or slide to the setup (Settings) application on your gadget
2. Select Security, followed by Screen lock
3. Select Swipe or None. Your safety prints will be erased as a consequence.

# Utilize your fingerprint

## Unlock or Decrypt your phone

1. For your phone to be unlocked, place your finger on the fingerprint sensor, which may be located on the display, power button, or the back of your device. To wake the display screen on some phones, tap the power button first
2. Sometimes, you'll need to utilize your backup Pincode, pattern, or passphrase to maintain security. This is necessary following:
   - After many attempts, your fingerprint is not recognized
   - Your phone is restarted (rebooted).
   - You change to another user
   - You last used your backup unlocking method more

# Unlock your gadget via face recognition

1. Via the lower section of the display screen, swipe upward

2. Click on the Settings app

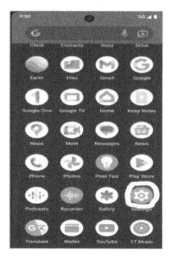

3. Select Privacy & Security

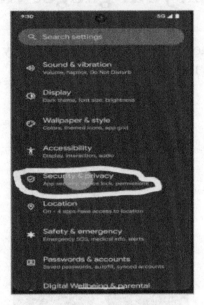

4. Select Lock device. Hit on Face or Facial & Fingerprint Unlock next

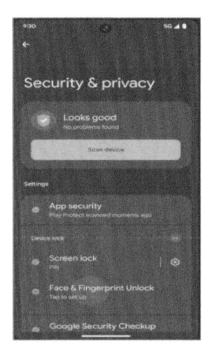

5. Click "Face Unlock."

97

6. Tap I agree to set Face or facial Unlock on your new gadget

7. Tap Start to start the enrolling process

8. To activate Face Unlock, position your face in the center of the circle while holding your smartphone at eye level. Then, slant your face upward and downward to add tiles to the circle

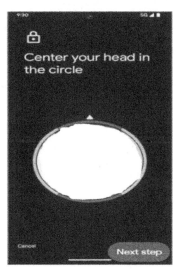

9. Click Done.

Note: Hold your phone in front of your face while pressing the power button to unlock it using face unlock.

## Configure Face Unlock

1. Navigate or slide to the setup  (Settings) application on your gadget
2. Then select Device Lock, followed by Facial & Finger or thumbprint Unlock, and afterward Face Unlock. Then select Safety & Privacy.
3. Put in your password, pattern, or PIN
4. Click Face Unlock, then click Review the details on the screen, then click I agree, and then click Start
5. Tap Done after following the on-screen directions.

## Set new Face Unlock parameters

With Facial Unlock activated:

- Navigate or slide to the setup  (Settings) application on your gadget
- Then select Device Lock, followed by Facial & Fingerprint Unlock, and afterward Face Unlock. Then select Safety & Privacy
- Insert in your passcode, Pincode, or pattern
- Click Face Unlock
- Deactivate the skip lock display screen.

# Remove facial data

You may erase face data to remove your facial model or disable Face Unlock.

With Facial Unlock activated:

1. Navigate or slide to the setup (Settings) application on your gadget
2. Then select Device Lock, followed by Facial & Fingerprint Unlock, and afterward Face Unlock. Then select Safety & Privacy
3. Put in your password, pattern, or PIN
4. Hit on Face or Facial Unlock
5. To delete a face model, choose Delete.

# Require open eyes

You may disable this Face Unlock function to unlock your new gadget even with your eyes closed.

With Facial Unlock activated:

1. Navigate or slide to the setup (Settings) application on your gadget
2. Then select Device Lock, followed by Face & Fingerprint Unlock, then Face Unlock. Then select Security & Privacy
3. Put in your password, pattern, or PIN
4. Click Face Unlock
5. Select "When using Face Unlock," then deactivate the checkbox next to Require eyes to be open.

# Password your new gadget

## Adding Password

1. Start the Settings program
2. Click the Security section here
3. Choose the screen lock you want to set by scrolling down to the Screen lock section.
4. Put the password in
5. Specify it once more
6. Next, choose the Done key from the notification options.

# CHAPTER 13

# Live Translation

## Configure Live Translation

1.  Navigate or slide to the setup (Settings) application on your gadget and select System
2.  Select Live Translate
3.  By default, Live Translate is enabled. Turn it on if it's off
4.  Tap Translate to select a different language to translate into
5.  Opt for a language
6.  The features that are supported in the language you choose will be listed for you. Choose or hit on language when ready
7.  Tap Add a language to add any more languages you wish to translate.

# Video and other media translation

## Chrome Lens

1. Open the Google Photos app to translate any languages that are visible in your screenshots or photos
2. Tap Lens after choosing a photo. Next, select Translate.

## Utilize Live Caption to translate speech to text

## Activate Live Caption

Live captioning is available in English, French, German, Italian, Japanese, and Spanish on Pixel 6 and Pixel 6 Pro smartphones.

You can also use auto-detection on Pixel 6 and Pixel 6 Pro phones to recognize these languages and translate media captions. Various other Android devices

## To enable or disable live captioning

1. Turn up the volume
2. Select Live Caption Live Caption Subtitles from the volume controls.

## Modifies the Live Caption settings

1. Navigate or slide to the setup (Settings) application on your gadget
2. Tap Live Caption, then Sound
3. You can discover or modify the popped-up preference under the options

# Type replies while on the phone

1. Open Settings on your phone to enable typing replies
2. Select Live Caption from the Accessibility menu
3. Enable typing responses while on calls
4. You are alerted when call captions are active during calls via a notice. Simply tap Keyboard Keyboard to begin typing.

# Translating via camera

## Utilize Live Translation

### Camera

1. Open your Camera app to use the translation feature to translate text you see on menus and signage
2. Select Translate from Modes > Lens.
3. Next, hold down the text you want to translate while tapping Translate.

# Text and voice translation on your gadget

## Activate Live Translation

1.  Navigate or slide to the setup (Settings) application on your gadget
2.  Select System, followed by Live Translate
3.  Use Live Translate is activated. By default, Live Translation will be toggled on.
4.  Setting a new default target language is optional
5.  Hit on translate to.
6.  Opt for a language
7.  Click Select Language
8.  Additional source languages are optional
9.  Select Add a language
10. Opt for a language
11. Click Select Language.

# Translating text

Some chat programs allow you to translate text messages while Live Translate is enabled. On-device translations are used for everything.

1.  Tap the language bubble to swap between the original language and the one you've selected.
2.  Changing your language preferences:
    *   Open a text discussion in the language of your choice
    *   Hit on the translation chip.
    *   Update the translation languages in the drop-down menu.

# To translate a solitary text:

1. Access a text message written in a different language
2. To select text, touch, and hold
3. Click Copy
4. Copy the write-ups & then hit on Translate.

**Tip: Tap the Drop-down menu to translate the entire page. Dropdown followed by full-page translation.**

# Utilize offline Live to Transcribe

## Install Language for offline usage

1. Open Live Transcribe on your device. Transcribing Live
2. Tap Settings Settings, followed by More Settings, towards the bottom
3. Surf to **Primary language and secondary language**

## Set your preferred offline mode.

1. Open Live Transcribe on your device. Transcribing Live
2. Tap Settings Settings, followed by More Settings, towards the bottom
3. Activate Transcribe offline.

# Message translation

1. Open a text message that is in a different language to translate it.
2. A request to download the new language will appear.
3. Reading translated text messages will thereafter be possible.

# Chapter 14

# Camera Guide

## Start the camera

o Press your phone's power button twice to access your camera from any screen.

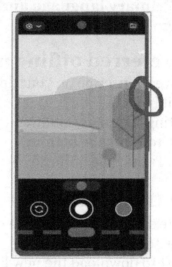

Note;

1. Go to Settings to enable this setting. Next,
2. select System > Gestures
3. open Camera swiftly

# Quick Tap

1. Tap your phone's back twice to access your camera from any screen.

Note: to enable quick tap

1. Open your Settings app to enable Quick Tap.
2. To begin an activity, tap System > Gestures > Quick Tap.
3. Set Use Quick Tap to on. After that, touch the Open app and select Camera.

# Flip your camera

1. Flip or Twist your phone twice when the Camera app is active to switch between the front and back camera

### To set the flip camera

1. Go to Settings to activate the Flip Camera for selfies. then
2. Select Flip camera for selfie under System > Gestures

Utilize functions like Night Sight and the video stabilization settings to take amazing photos and films.

# Settings

To activate face retouching, change the mode to Portrait. Next, select Settings from the dropdown menu by tapping it or by swiping down from the top of your screen. The next options are to utilize flash, set a timer, or activate face retouching.

# Night Sight

The greatest colors and features that are hidden in the dark are brought out by Night Sight.

1. Hit on Night Sight, then
2. Hit on Capture to capture a picture while using the Night Sight feature.

# Long or Extended Exposure

Motion enables you to artistically blur your images.

1. Tap Long Exposure to capture a blurry image of a moving object

# Blur

You will be able to use picture blur to alter the focus of your image.

1. Scroll to Tools,
2. Choose Portrait Blur, and then
3. Select Blur when editing a photo.
   - To switch the region of focus and modify the slider as necessary, tap the screen.

# Record

1. Tap Video to start a recording.
2. Tap Record to begin recording after that.

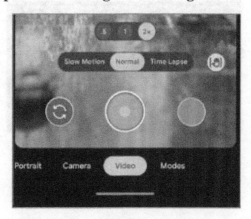

# Edit a picture

## Modify the picture format

By default, your camera stores picture files in a JPEG layout. Additionally, you may store your camera's pictures in RAW format as supplementary files.

## To enable JPEG + RAW files:

1. Launch the Camera app
2. Press the Down arrow, then select Settings
3. Select Advanced.
4. Set the RAW+JPEG control to on.

## Utilizing RAW files

Take a picture in default or Night Sight mode.

1. Navigate to your gadget's Home screen
2. Slide upward via the lower section of the display screen to navigate utilizing gestures
3. Two or three buttons for navigation: Tap "Home."
4. Activate Google Photos
5. Tap Raw, then Library, on the bottom right.

# Utilizing Google Photos' Magic Eraser

1. Start your phone's Google Photos app
2. Locate the image you intend to edit using the Magic Eraser tool. The main screen of the Google Picture application under the Photos app will display the images taken using the Camera app.

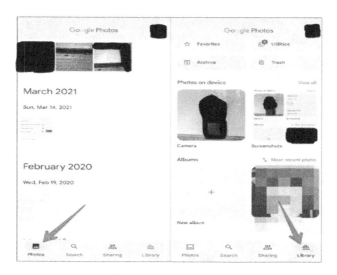

- To see the available albums if you're looking for earlier pictures, such as screenshots or WhatsApp images, tap on the Library preference (option) at the lower section of the screen. then launch the chosen picture.

3. Press the Edit icon. Click on the Tools option after scrolling through the list of available tools at the bottom. Go to the Magic Eraser not available section via the ending of the post if you can't see Tools.

4. After that, select Magic Eraser. Google Photos will look for the undesirable parts and recommend them. Tap the items to eliminate them if you wish to follow the recommendations. To pick an item, you may also use your finger to sketch a rounded shape around it or to brush over it.

5. Immediately you raise your finger, Google Pictures will erase the chosen object using its magic. Use your finger to pick any other items you want to get rid of or delete. To undo the modifications if you don't want the filled background, hit on the rear knob (button) at the lower section.

6. As an alternative, select Camouflage and use your finger to sketch the item at the lower section to blend the undesirable thing into your image

7. Hit on **Done** once you are pleased with the result. You'll arrive at Google Photos' primary editing page, where you may make more

changes to your image. Then choose Save as Copy. View the top Google Photos picture editing advice.

# Fixing malfunctioning Magic Eraser or not Being Available

Try the following remedies if the Magic Eraser crashes or doesn't appear.

### Phone update

The software on your phone has to be checked and updated as well. Navigate or slide to setup (Settings) > System > Software update to do that.

# How to Use the Pixel 8's Magic Eraser

## Use a magic eraser to get rid of the unwanted items

1. On your new pixel gadget, launch the Google Picture application.
2. Hit a photo to bring it up in full-screen mode, then hit Edit

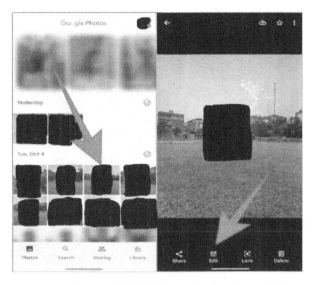

3. Tap Tools or slide leftward via the editing mode menu. After that, tap Magic Eraser to continue

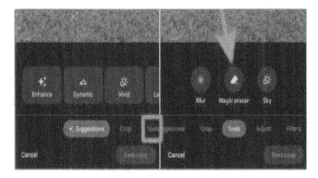

4. After the Magic Eraser has finished loading, use your finger to rub the area around the thing you wish to erase from the picture. And immediately you remove your finger from the display screen, it will be deleted

5. Tap Done after editing is finished. Click Save Copy to store the picture in Google Photos after that.

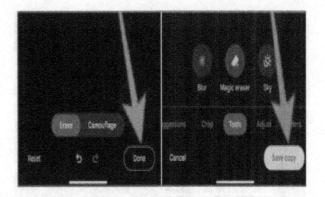

## Magic Eraser for audio

1. Choose the layer-separating audio magic erase icon once the phone analyses the sound
2. You may then enter and modify the volume levels of various sound components to obtain the ideal blend.

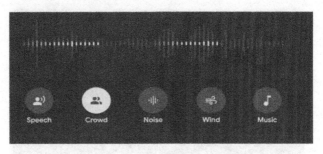

# Crop, resize, or align a picture

## Straighten pictures with gridlines

1. Tap the Down arrow on the Camera app
2. After selecting More Settings, tap Grid type
3. Choose the grid type that you desire.

## Change the photo's aspect ratio.

1. Tap the Down arrow on the Camera app
2. Choose from the wide crop and full picture ratio options.

# Crop a picture

1. Go to the picture you wish to modify in the Photos app
2. Select Crop from the Edit Photo menu.
3. You may resize the borders to the size you want.

# Adjust the color, brightness, or blur of a picture

Within the Photos app:

1. Check out the picture you intended to modify
2. Select Tools, then Edit
3. From here, you may change a photo's lighting, color, or blur.

## Picture unblur

Photo Unblur can help you fix fuzzy photos.

1. Launch the Photos application.
2. Click the picture you intended to modify

3. Select Edit Photo, Tools, and Unblur from the menu.

# Remove or reduce unwanted items or elements from a photograph

1. Go to the picture you wish to modify in the Photo application
2. Touch Edit, followed by Tools and Magic eraser.
3. On a suggestion, tap. The round or brush can be used to remove further distractions from the image
4. Hit on Camouflage and utilize the brush to make items blend in with the background of the picture
5. Tap Done to complete.

# Take portrait pictures

1. Launch the Google Camera program
2. Select Portrait, then select Capture
3. Hit on the picture in the lower right corner to see the improved version.

# Find, remove, or save a picture or movie

Via Google Picture installed on your phone gadget, you may remove, save, or locate a picture or a movie.

## Removing photographs and videos

1. Via your Android device, launch the Google Picture application.

2. Register by scrolling to your Account.
3. To move a picture or film (video) to the trash, tap and hold it. There are various options available
4. Tap Trash Delete at the top.

## Save your images or videos.
1. Via your Android device, launch the Google Picture application.
2. Select & hit on a photograph or a video
3. Click More, followed by Download.

## Locate your pictures and videos

To locate your pictures:

1. Launch the Google Picture application
2. Click Photos.

## Share images and videos

You will be able to share the pictures, films, albums, & movies of whichever of your contacts with them even when they do not utilize the Google Photographs app.

## Share movies and images during a discussion
1. Navigate to photos.google.com on your PC
2. Slide to your Account & sign in
3. Select Done by moving your mouse over a picture or a video
4. To share, click Share
5. Choose whoever you want to share photos with under "Send in Google Photos."
6. Hit on the individual name you would prefer to share with

7. Click Search to discover a certain individual. Type in their name, and contact information, such as a phone number or email address
8. Click New Group, pick several individuals to share with, and then click Share
9. Google proposes recipients of your sharing based on your interactions to make it simpler.
   - **Optional: To go with your shared media, write a note.**
10. Select Send.

## Generate a shared photo album.

1. Navigate to photos.google.com on your PC
2. Navigate or Sign in by sliding into your Google Account.
3. Click Photos on the left
4. Select Done by moving your mouse over a picture or a video
5. Click Create New Add or Add at the top
6. Select New Shared Album after selecting Shared album
7. Input the name or designation of an album
8. Hit on the Share icon via the upper right angle.
9. Click Send Send after choosing who you want to send the album to.

# Share or send a link using other applications

1. Navigate to photos.google.com on your PC
2. Select Done by moving your mouse over a picture or a video.
3. Simply click Share to email a link
4. Pick a sharing method for your link.

5. Hit on **the Create link** so you will be able to share
6. Choose the app you wish to use to share content through other applications.

# Manage, review, or delete your discussions and albums

## Discover shared albums and chats

1. Navigate to photos.google.com on your PC
2. Hit on **Sharing** via the upper left angle. Your shared albums, chats, and sharing activity, such as comments and recently uploaded photographs, are all available
3. If you can't find what you're searching for, click Show More at the bottom.

## Exit an album

1. Go to the album
2. Click More More in the upper right corner, followed by Leave album.

## Exit a conversation.

1. Click the dialogue
2. Click your account symbol or initial in the chat
3. Click Leave next to your name to exit.

# Remove individuals or items from discussions and albums.

## Delete a person from the album

1. Open the album where you wish to delete a person
2. Select Options after clicking More More
3. Check for the contact you intended to erase via sliding or scrolling.
4. Then click More More Remove the individual.

## Delete the images and videos

1. Click on the image or video in the chat thread or a shared album
2. Click More More and then Remove in the upper right corner.

## Delete likes and comments

1. Click on the remark or like in a shared album or chat thread
2. Press Delete.

# CHAPTER 15

# Split Screen

## Get split-screen access

1. Slide upward via the lower section of the screen while keeping your finger on it to see recently used applications

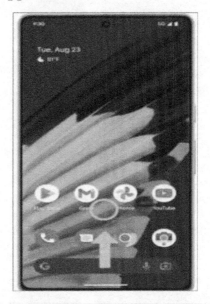

2. After choosing the desired program icon, choose Split Top.

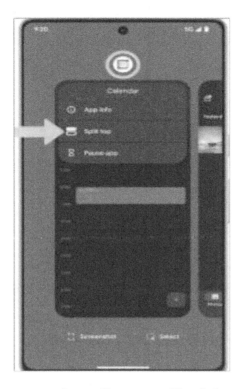

- **Note that Split screen will only be available in supported apps.**

3. Choose whatever application you intend to see in the bottom pane. To switch the bottom app, slide upward via the lower section of the display screen while keeping your finger on the screen

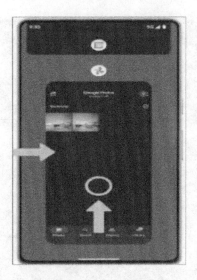

- **Note: The Photo and Calendar apps were utilized for this example.**

# Resize the windows

The Divider symbol in the center of the screen should be selected and moved up or down as needed, then released.

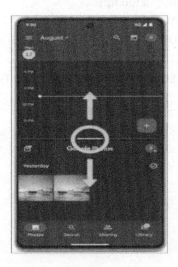

# Close the split-screen window

From the bottom of the screen, swipe up while holding. To close the split-screen window, swipe it upward.

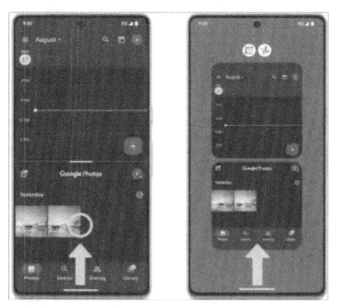

# Utilize picture-in-picture

Slide upward via the lower section of the display screen while using a fullscreen app like Google Maps, browser, video applications, etc. In the screen's corner, the app will appear as a Picture-in-Picture window

- **Note: The window may be chosen and moved as needed. On a few applications, picture-in-picture is turned on by default. Swipe down from the notification bar with two fingers to reveal the settings icon. Select applications & notifications > Advanced > Special app access > Picture-in-picture. This will reveal the list of applications that support Picture-in-Picture.**

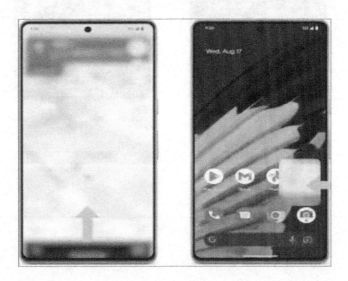

# CHAPTER 16

# Screen hacks and videos

## Recording your gadgets Screen

1. First, we'll make sure the screen recording icon is there on the Google Pixel 8 Pro's fast access panel. (If we have it already, scroll to the next phase)

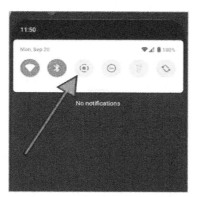

- To examine it, we unlock our Pixel 8 Pro and move our finger down a few centimeters from the top edge of the display screen to reveal the fast panel. Here, the quick settings, like turning on Bluetooth, turning on Wi-Fi, turning on mute, turning on airplane mode, etc., will be displayed.

- Once the complete panel has been displayed by sliding down once again with one finger, look to see if the symbol for screen recording is present:

2. Click on the edit icon of the quick panel, which is typically represented by a pencil, if you do not the screen displays the recording logo on your Gadget

3. The settings icons that we may add to the Google Pixel 8 Pro fast panel will appear above and below the settings icons that we have already specified in the quick panel, separated by a horizontal line.

- We locate the screen display recording logo, hit on it, and then drag it up to the upper section to include it in the fast panel without releasing it.

4. There are 2 methods to begin recording at this point. One is to quickly unfold the panel by sliding a finger from the top of the screen and pressing the screen recording icon that we have seen in the previous steps. The other is more straightforward and less likely to go wrong.

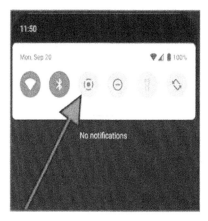

5. In this step, you may decide whether or not you want the video to be stored with sound and if you want to display the screen's touch input. Choose the choices that appeal to you.

6. By selecting the "Record audio" drop-down option, you can decide whether you want both the device audio and the microphone sound to be captured simultaneously in the video

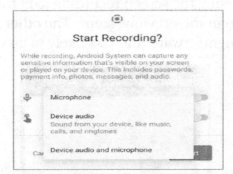

7. The Google Pixel 8 Pro screen will display a 3-second countdown, after which video of everything that occurs on the screen will begin to be recorded.

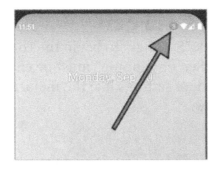

8. Hit on the Gadget's upward volume & power knobs must be pressed simultaneously once more to stop recording. Alternatively, you may click "Stop" in the upper left or right corner of the screen.

The movie will be instantly saved to your Pixel 8 gadget picture gallery. The picture arcade or gallery is positioned on the home display screen.

# Pinning a screen

1. We pick "Settings" to begin the configuration since "Screen pinning" must be enabled from the Gadget settings like the majority of Android features.

2. Next, find the "Security" area in the Google Pixel 8 Pro settings by scrolling down and clicking.

3. This requires us to choose "Advanced" to access the Google Pixel 8 Pro settings, which hide the pin screen function.

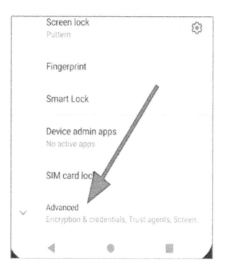

Screen lock
Pattern

Fingerprint

Smart Lock

Device admin apps
No active apps

SIM card loc

Advanced
Encryption & credentials, Trust agents, Screen...

4. Select the "Screen pinning" area by scrolling down the Google Pixel 8 Pro screen and pressing it to bring it up and customize its settings.

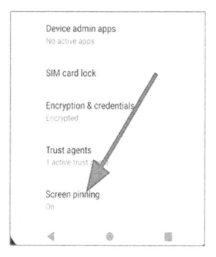

Device admin apps
No active apps

SIM card lock

Encryption & credentials
Encrypted

Trust agents
1 active trust agent

Screen pinning
On

5. If "Screen pinning" is not already active, press to make it so.

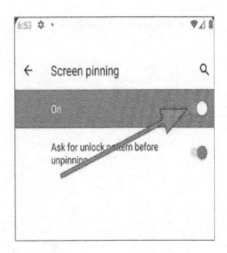

6. In the sixth step, you may safeguard your unique unlock code or pattern by selecting "Ask for unlock pattern before unpinning" if you want to use a different code from the one you used to unlock the Google Pixel 8 Pro.

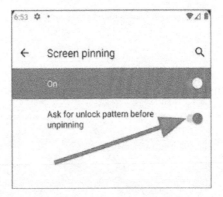

7. We've previously turned on this really useful feature to lend someone else the Google Pixel 8 Pro. The application you want to "pin" or keep open from which you won't be able to exit without unlocking the Pixel 8 Pro must first be launched. Once it has been launched, you must

click on the Recent Applications button, which is located in the bottom right corner of your Pixel 8 Pro's screen.

8. The menu of potential options will now appear when you click on the icon of the program you want to **"pin on the screen"**

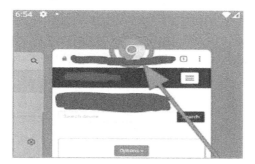

9. You will notice "Pin" next to the icon of a thumbtack or tack among the alternatives that will now be presented. To pin this app to your Gadget, hit on it.

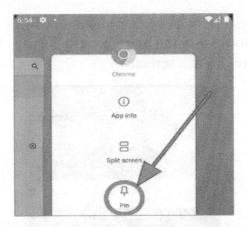

10. Anyone using your Gadget will be unable to quit the program without knowing the unlock code or pattern that you have established because the application is already stuck on the screen. When done, hit on & hold the rear and recent applications buttons simultaneously as shown in the image below if you want to deactivate or stop configuring this application.

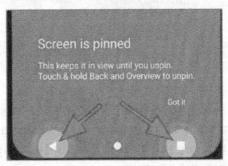

# Scanning document

1.  Find the Google Drive application on your new gadget. It should be on the home screen or in the applications menu if you have never used it. If you can't find it on your home display screen, you will be able to search for and download it from the Play Store or search for it in the "Google" folder.

2.  After that, Google Drive will urge you to sign in using your Google (account) if you are opening it for the first time. You may use the Google account that you use for your new Gadget. You should hit on the "plus" knob (button) positioned at the lower right of the display screen.

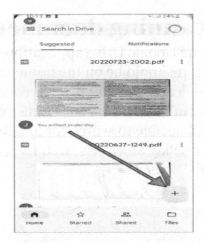

3. The third step is to select "Scan" from the menu that will display at the bottom of the screen. To begin document scanning with your Pixel 8 Pro, tap it.

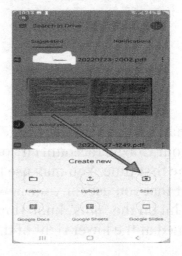

4. Using your newest Gadget's camera, focus on the document to make sure it fills the center of the screen and can be seen clearly in step four. When you're ready, press the camera's capture button.

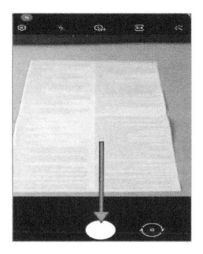

5. Check the taken image to make sure it is defined and the text can be read. If everything is okay, click "Accept," otherwise, click "Retry."

6. Using the icons that appear at the lower section of the screen, you may rotate or flip, crop, retouch the colors, or add new photographs to the document capture so you may able to add

them via a similar PDF. If everything is accurate, press "Save" to proceed

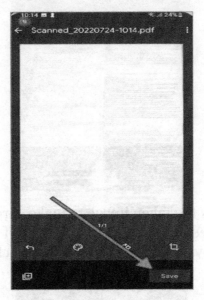

7. In the following stage, you may select the name, Google account, and folder under which you wish the PDF file to be saved. This is the seventh step. When you have finished configuring everything, click "Save" in the bottom right corner of your Gadgets display screen.

8. Your document has already been scanned and stored as a PDF in both your Google Drive account and the new Pixel 8 Pro's internal storage. You may find it by exploring the folders or using the search engine that displays at the top. Once the file is discovered, click on the three vertical dots that appear on its right side if you want to transmit it by email or a messaging service

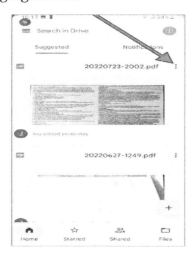

9. You will get a menu of options for this document. You may share it directly with other Google Drive users or send a copy of it. To send a copy of the document by email or message, select the "Send a copy" option.

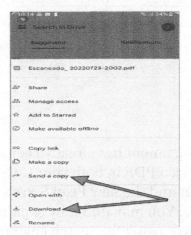

10. By selecting "Send a copy," the operating system's choices menu for sending or sharing files will display. From there, use WhatsApp, Telegram, Gmail, Bluetooth, or any other accessible program to share the scanned document.

# Reading QR codes

You may use the following to scan QR codes:

- using the camera
- using Google

## Via the camera

1.  We will utilize the Google Pixel 8 Pro's rear camera and the official software that comes pre-installed to read QR codes.

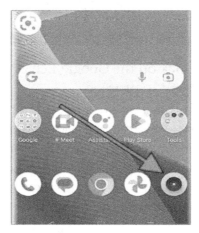

- It is typically a camera symbol or a camera lens, so look for it on the home screen or in the apps menu.

2.  Launch the camera application on your Pixel 8 Pro. You will see an icon in the lower-left corner of the image that is recorded by the camera, as seen in the accompanying image and denoted by an arrow.

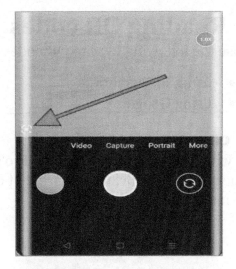

- Click on the Google Lens symbol if you want to proceed
- If this icon does not pop up, keep reading to learn about your options.

3. If this is your first time using Google Lens on your newest Gadget, a notice will be shown informing you that you must grant the app permission to use the camera

4. At this point, we have the option of allowing
   Google Lens to utilize the device's camera
   whenever it is open, asking every time it is
   opened, or not asking at all.

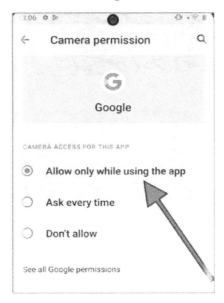

- To scan QR codes on our Google Pixel 8
  Pro, we must pick one of the first two
  possibilities. After selecting an option,
  hit on the rear knob (button) to go back
  to the Google Lens app.

5. Using the Google Lens app on the Pixel 8 Pro,
   make sure the rear camera is on and point it at
   the QR code you want to read, trying to get it to
   appear properly focused and contained within
   the square, or at least within the display space.
   Be careful not to get too close to the code to
   avoid it being cut off or becoming blurry.

- Since the QR code has no top or bottom and must be completely visible on the Pixel 8 Pro display screen, it does not matter how we approach it.

6. Following the QR code's scanning, a message will show up and give us the option to take action. Since most QR codes contain a web address, it will suggest that we open the default web browser on our Google Pixel 8 Pro.

- To open the website or run the QR code action, click on the notice or the magnifying glass.

## Through Google

1. If you have the Google search engine widget on your Google Pixel 8 Pro's home screen, click the camera symbol that displays to the right of the search box. If you have the Google Lens app installed, you can also search for it here

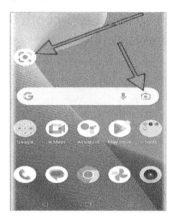

2. Open the Chrome browser or the Google program, as seen in the image below, if you don't already have the Google widget on your home screen

3. Pressing the camera icon that displays to the right of the search box in both the Chrome web browser and the Google app is the third step.

4. The Google Lens app will launch in the fourth step, after which you can go back to step 3 of this guide.

# CHAPTER 17

# Capturing your screen & taking screenshots on your gadget

The ability to take screenshots, or record a snapshot of what is now visible on the screen of your Google Pixel 8 Pro, is a crucial function of contemporary mobile phones and tablets

First approach

- The screenshot-taking without pressing the buttons
- Capture or record a whole page?

**First approach:**

You must adhere to these easy steps to snap a screenshot on your Pixel 8:

1. Go to the web page, conversation, or program on your Pixel 8 Pro that you wish to snap a screenshot of first.

2. Hit the power & downward volume knob (buttons) on your Pixel 8 Pro simultaneously. The process is the same, except you must hit the volume up key and the power key simultaneously to record a video.

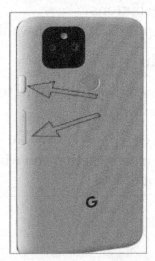

3. Your mobile/cell phone's gallery is automatically updated with the taken image.

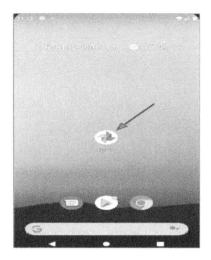

- Google Pictures or Photos could be your image gallery program; in that case, search for the logo of a paper 4-pointed star with 4 colors, one for each point. You can check out the picture arcade or gallery via the home display screen; there should be a photograph logo, an instantaneous picture, or base on the software model downloaded

4. When you click on the screenshot that was just taken on your Pixel 8 Pro, you can now edit, crop, or share it with your friends or through your favorite social network.

- Navigate to & launch the picture arcade (gallery). The pictures and photographs will be displayed in order by date.

# Screenshot-taking without pressing the buttons

1. Go to the program or screen you wish to capture with your Google.
2. Show your Google Pixel 8 Pro's quick access or settings bar. The shortcuts to the device settings will be shown if you move your finger down from the top of the screen to do this.

3. Press the screenshot icon. If the symbol is not
   visible, slide down again to show the complete
   panel

4. Google immediately saves the captured
   photograph in your phone or tablet's gallery.

Google Photos may be your image gallery program; in
that case, search for the icon of a 4-pointed star made
of paper with four colors, one for each point. You will
be able to check out the picture arcade or gallery via
the home display screen; there should be a picture
logo, an instantaneous picture, or base on the
software model installed

# Capture or record a whole page

Use the approach described above to take a screenshot while scrolling on a website, a WhatsApp chat, or any other program on your Google Pixel 8 Pro. The screenshot menu will briefly show at the bottom once the screenshot has been taken.

- Click the "Capture more" button before it vanishes to bring up an editing menu where you may choose how much of the screen to capture
- Once the capture has been done, it will be saved in the image gallery of the Pixel 8 Pro, where you may modify and share it with others.

# CHAPTER 18

# Emergency

# Set up the emergency calls

Only devices with a SIM or eSIM card may be
configured to make emergency calls since they utilize
the call service over the GSM network. If that is not
feasible, the device must be linked to a Wi-Fi network,
through Bluetooth, to another device that has a GSM
connection, or to the Internet.

1. Let's get to the new Pixel 8 series settings. You
   can do this by tapping the gear-wheel symbol
   on the device's home screen.

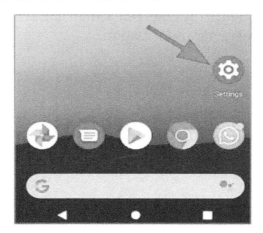

2. Next, we navigate to the final menu item under
   "Information about the device" in the new Pixel
   8 settings. Access by clicking it.

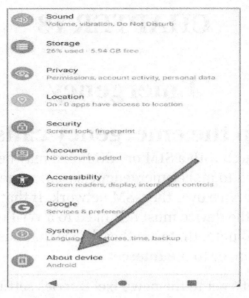

3. The Pixel 8 series name, model, and phone number will be displayed in the third stage. To configure the emergency data, click "Emergency information."

- If it doesn't show up here, return or navigate back & access the "Security" area; depending on the operating system version, it could show up somewhere else.

4. In the "Emergency Information" area of the fourth stage, we may enter the information that we intended to see on the Google Pixel 8 Pro screen if the **SOS** mode is enabled.

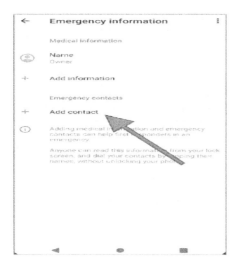

- This is helpful, for instance, in the case of an incident, so that the **SOS** services will be aware of the device owner's critical medical information and will get in touch with them or their loved ones. To add contacts for emergencies, click "Add contact".

5. Find the contacts you wish to be warned about emergencies in your Google Pixel 8 Pro phonebook, and then click on each one to add them

6. Add the remaining information you wish to the emergency screen by clicking "Add information" in the sixth step. Viewing this data is possible without having access to the Google Pixel 8 Pro's PIN, pattern, or access password.

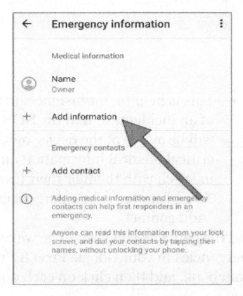

7. Add your name, address (important in case of loss), blood type, allergies, medications, and other medical information at this stage. You'll be done setting up the contacts for SOS emergency calls on your Google Pixel 8 Pro once you've added this information.

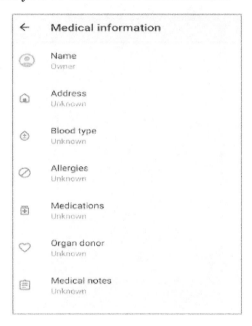

# Sending an SOS call

1. Touch & hold the Pixel 8 Pro's power knob (button) for some seconds until the restart or shutdown screen appears to access data and emergency contacts

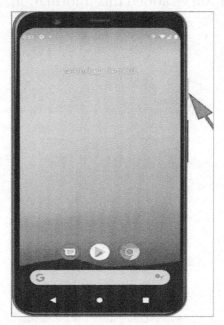

2. There will be three choices: Reboot, Shutdown, and Emergency. To view the options for emergency calls and SOS contacts, choose "Emergency"

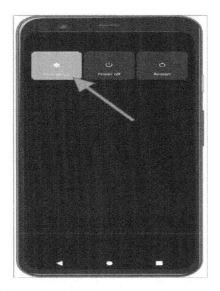

3. A keyboard and a button at the top that reads "EMERGENCY INFORMATION" will show on your Google Pixel 8 Pro's screen. To access the emergency information that the device's owner has defined, click this button

4. The Pixel 8 owner's information will be shown, along with emergency contacts. You may call someone without entering a PIN, pattern, fingerprint, or password by pressing the call icon that displays to the right of each contact.

# Delete any emergency details

1. Touch & hold the new Pixel 8 power knob (button) for some seconds until the restart or shutdown screen appears to access data and emergency contacts
2. There will be three choices: Reboot, Shutdown, and Emergency. To view the options for emergency calls and SOS contacts, choose "Emergency"
3. A keyboard and a button at the top that reads "EMERGENCY INFORMATION" will show on your Pixel 8 Pro's screen. To access the emergency information that the device's owner has defined, click this button
4. Once within the emergency information, we may click the owner's information to modify it

171

and then hit the X to remove the emergency contacts.

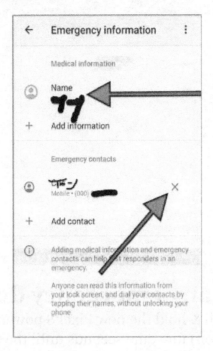

# Activate or turn off safe mode

Only a few system applications can function in safe mode, which is a functioning mode for Android gadgets in which user-downloaded and user-installed applications are disabled.

The goal of safe mode is fixing issues that may be brought on by downloaded programs. It is a straightforward and practical technique to determine whether any application placed on your handset is creating system faults as well as identify potential viral info.

You can snap a screenshot before going into safe mode to restore the widgets that were deleted when you activated safe mode because doing so would also remove them from the screen.

You can go back to the standard mode & delete any recently installed programs to see if any of them are the root of the issues if you use safe mode to confirm that the device functions correctly.

Before enabling or disabling safe mode, you should be aware that since the device will restart, you'll need the SIM card's PIN as well as the unlock code or pattern.

# Switch on safe mode

1. Simply hold down the power knob (button) pending when the next screen with power off, restart, and emergency mode preference displays to enter safe mode

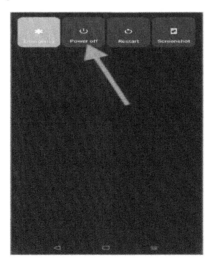

2. When prompted to start the device in safe mode, hit "OK" after pressing and holding the "Power off" symbol.

# Turn off the safe mode

It is quite easy to exit safe mode;

1. Simply press and hold the power button on the gadget until the screen with the options for restart, shutdown, and emergency mode displays.
2. Hit on restart

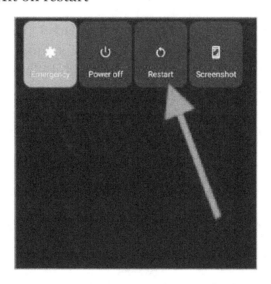

# Set up the heads-up display MODE to prevent collisions

If the function detects that you are walking while using your phone, it will regularly show a reminder to pay attention to your surroundings.

1. Go to Digital Safety or Wellbeing & Parental Controls > Heads Up in Settings
2. After selecting Next, allow Heads Up access to your location and movement information
3. Press Next and then Done to complete setting up the function.

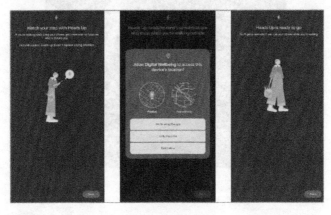

# Switch to one-handed mode

You must first enable one-handed mode

# Enable one-handed mode

1. Navigate or slide to setup (Settings) > System > Gestures >
2. Now hit on One-handed mode before you can utilize it.

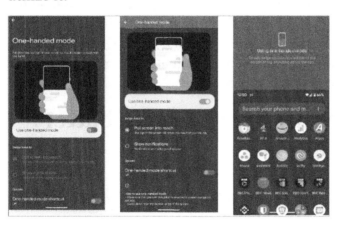

## Utilize a shortcut to activate one-handed mode

- You must swipe down towards the bottom border or edge of the screen to activate the mode.
- Hit on the one-handed mode icon to activate it

# CHAPTER 19

## Common Issues with the Google Pixel 8 Pro and Solutions

The most frequent difficulties that your Google Pixel phone could have are mentioned in the section below, along with the most popular fix that can be used to fix them without professional assistance or a trip to the Google Pixel repair facility.

## Facing an excessive battery drain issue

- To check screen time, navigate to settings →Battery →Show complete device use.
- From the settings menu, disable the automatic brightness option.
- Uncheck the box under Apps in Settings→ Show Unused App Notifications
- Disable Bluetooth, GPS, Wi-Fi, and mobile hotspot
- Keep screen time to one minute or less.
- Examine the latest official software upgrades
- Limit the phone's charge.

# Stuck, frozen, and unresponsive screens

1. Simply click the Power knob ( button) to restart your phone.
2. You may start your new gadget in Safe Mode as well
3. To adequately inspect the screen, download and install the Display Tester app
4. The gadget will need to be factory reset as the last step.

# The Google Pixel 8 Pro won't boot up

- To power off the phone and restart it, long press the Power + Volume Up buttons.
- You should try to boot or power up into safe mode
- Get the most current firmware update
- Delete the phone's cache partition
- Utilize Hard Reset to completely erase the data.
- Visit the Google Pixel care center closest to you.

# Problem with Overheating

- Use the original Google Pixel charger and avoid overcharging the gadget
- By selecting and then performing the restart procedure, you may restart the computer
- When not utilized, toggle GPS, Wi-Fi & Bluetooth off
- Close all unused background program
- Now check out for a system update.

# Wi-Fi connectivity issues

1. Restarting the computer will update the connection settings
2. Ensure you are within Wi-Fi range
3. Wi-Fi network disconnect, then rejoin
4. Any issues with the router or modem should be changed
5. The Wi-Fi connection cable should be properly inspected
6. You might also try to reset the network settings.

## How to Fix Google Pixel 8 Pro Constant WiFi Disconnection

You can attempt the next technique if the Wi-Fi keeps disconnecting even after you've reset the network settings.

- Press & hold to select Wi-Fi.
- The chosen network's Settings button should be selected
- Choose the View More option
- Change the IP setting from DHCP to static.
- Try reconnecting to your favorite network once again.

# Whenever Applications via the Google Play Store refuse to Download

How Can I Fix The Problem Where The Google Pixel 8 Pro Won't Install Or Update Apps?

- Confirm or Check the Internet connection's speed.
- To solve this issue, restart the gadget
- Clear data and the cache by going to Settings Apps Google Play Store Storage
- You must Force Stop the Google Play Store app if the previous step doesn't resolve the issue
- Activate Automatic date and time under Settings General Management Date and time
- Verify the amount of internal storage on the device
- Sign in using your primary Gmail account after deleting all other Google accounts.

# Google Pixel 8 Pro Bluetooth Issues

How to Fix the Google Pixel 8 Pro's Bluetooth Pairing Issue?

- Slide the notification bar downward, turn Bluetooth off, and then turn it back on
- Turn off the Aeroplane Mode and enable it from the notification panel.
- Your Google Pixel 8 Pro should restart once
- Restart the device search after disabling the pairing

- Select Bluetooth, Storage, Clean Cache, Bluetooth, Apps, Filter Options, and Show System Apps from the Settings menu
- Verify the compatibility of the gadget with your phone
- Try to establish a Bluetooth or smartphone connection.
- A reset of the network settings is another option you should try out
- Install the most recent firmware revision.

# Text Messages Aren't Sending

Repairing the Google Pixel 8 Pro Can't send text messages (SMS)?

1. Restart your device first
2. Make sure the SIM is correctly inserted
3. Verify the cellular connection
4. Verify if outbound SMS service is offered under the carrier plan
5. Tap Force Stop after giving the Message App a long tap
6. Delete the cache and data for the messaging app
7. To send text messages quickly, reset the network settings
8. Contact your service provider if the aforementioned approach doesn't work.

# Delete the data and cache in the Message App

1. Click & grip the Message App
2. Click on App Info.
3. Toggle to the Storage→ Delete Cache and Data

# Google Pixel 8 Pro Network Issue

How can I fix my Google Pixel 8 Pro's internet problem?

- Restart your Google Pixel 8 Pro mobile device.
- To reset the networks, re-insert the SIM card.
- Activate and deactivate the Aeroplane mode to temporarily block networks
- To prevent access from third-party apps, enter Safe Mode
- Reset the network connection's configuration.

outlined are some more complex preferences.

## Verify the device's network settings

1. Launch the Settings app
2. Navigate to Network & Internet
3. Hit on Mobile Network
4. More advanced Toggle on "Automatically choose network" by looking for it there.

## Disable "Roaming mode"

1. Click the Settings button
2. Hit on Mobile Network service below Network & web (Internet)
3. Eliminate the "Roaming" checkbox.

# Issues with the Google Pixel 8 Pro camera

How Can Google Pixel 8 Pro Camera Issues Be Fixed?

- Hit on Settings (setup) via the menu
- Decide on App management
- Find the Camera app
- Scroll or slide to the Storage preference
- Hit on Clear Data & Cache
- Return and select Force Stop
- Find the most recent Android update
- Phone factory reset.

# Google Pixel 8 Pro Stopped Turning On Suddenly

How to Fix the Google Pixel 8 Pro That Randomly Turns Off?

- Look for any material or software issues to the phone
- By holding down the Volume Downward knob & the Power knob, you may force a restart
- If it doesn't work, try charging the device first before attempting a Force Restart.

# Google Pixel 8 Pro Restarts Constantly

1. Start the gadget in safe mode
2. Connect to the charger and restart your phone manually
3. For a seamless experience, reset all of the settings.

4. Also, try out a Factory Reset.

# Google Pixel 8 Pro Ghost Touch Issue

How Can the Google Pixel 8 Pro Fix Ghost Touch?

- You might try restarting your device
- To prevent inadvertent touching, remove the rear cover
- Accidental touch protection may be enabled in the display settings
- Turn off touch sensitivity in the display settings
- Swipe movements should replace the Navigation bar
- All system programs or apps must be updated.
- Seek out the latest software patch.
- And lastly, factory reset the gadget.

# GPS Issues on your gadget (Pixel)

How Can the Pixel 8 Pro's GPS Problem Be Fixed?

- Activate and deactivate the GPS position button
- You will be able to toggle Airplane Mode on/off
- Power Saving mode should be disabled
- Select High accuracy mode under Settings Location Mode
- Clear Google Maps' data and cache.

# Slow Charging on your gadget

How Can the Pixel 8 Pro's Slow Charging Problem Be Fixed?

- Substitute with a fresh charger.
- Take out any objects that are blocking the charging port.
- Update your operating system for consistent charging
- Make sure you are utilizing the genuine Type-C cable.
- For quicker charging, just utilize the original Charger.
- Verify whether the port is damaged.
- Alternate or use a different power outlet.

# Crashing & freezing Applications

How can I repair the app freezing issue on my Google Pixel 8 Pro?

- Force Your Google Pixel 8 Pro phone should restart
- Be certain you are using the newest OS version.
- Select the app that is frozen under Apps, then go to Settings Apps Storage Clear Cache & Data
- Try a factory reset if the previous step doesn't work.

# CHAPTER 20

# Common Steps for Google Pixel Devices in Troubleshooting

## Start (Re-launch) your gadget
1. Press the power button repeatedly
2. Choose Restart from the menu.

## Hard-resetting your gadget
1. Press and hold the Power key and the Volume Down key for 10 seconds.

## Launch Safe Mode on your Google Pixel 8 Pro
1. Hold the power knob down for a few seconds
2. Choose Safe Mode from the menu.

## Using Gadget (Pixel) backup data
1. Navigate to Accounts & Backup under Settings
2. Click on Data backup
3. Select Google One Backup from the menu
4. Select the desired Gmail account in the upper right corner.

# Factory reset gadget

1. Activate the Settings menu
2. Opt for General Management
3. Select Reset by tapping it
4. Reset factory data Click Reset
5. Press Delete all to finish.

# Resetting your gadget's network settings

1. Activate the Settings app
2. Press the General Management button
3. Select Reset by clicking
4. Reset Settings Reset Network Settings
5. Finally, press the Reset and Confirm button.

# Erase the cache partition

1. To switch off the phone, long press the Downward Volume + Power knob
2. The Volume Up + Power key should then be pressed and held
3. When the Google Pixel logo shows, release all buttons
4. Use the Volume keys to navigate, and the Power key to choose to clear the cache sector
5. Select Reboot System Now after that

It's all done now!

# Conclusion

It's important to note that the Pixel 8 now has a 6.2-inch screen and refreshes at 120Hz, while the 8 device Pro retains its 6.8-inch size and slightly larger aspect ratio of 20:9 (as opposed to 19.5:9). These devices now possess a whole lot of features which makes a huge upgrade

# BOOK INDEX

Made in the USA
Monee, IL
28 October 2023